SHADOW BIRDS
by
S.M. Minish

OPEN GATE PRESS
LONDON

Published in 2010 by Open Gate Press
51 Achilles Road, London NW6 1DZ

British Library Cataloguing-in-Publication Programme
A catalogue reference for this book is available from the
British Library.

ISBN: 978-1-871871-71-5

p. 49 'Salad Bowl' was published under the title 'Call to a Simple Feast' in
Opening eyes – a poetry collection – by Cambridge University Press, 2010.
p. 2 'Voyaging' was first published in *Agenda*, Spring issue 2008.
p. 28 'Retreat' won first prize in the Crann Poetry Competition 2001.
p. 1 'Ice Core Sample', p. 7 'Sound', p. 35 'Failed Diplomacy',
p. 37 'Mare' and p. 45 'Last Prisoner of War', were first published in
Beyond the Reek – An Anthology of Eleven Mayo Poets, Westport, 2000.
p. 8 'Salix [Willows]', p. 44 'Stolen Curiosities', p. 51 'Pentecostal Wind in
Jerusalem' and p. 54 'Moonrise', were first published in
Tidal Dreams – An Anthology of Seven Poets, Mayo, 1996.
p. 14 'Lichen' was first published in *Under the Shadow – An Anthology*
in 1992.

Cover illustration by S.M. Minish

Printed and bound in Great Britain by Imprint Digital, Exeter, Devon

After finishing school in England S.M. Minish attended the University of Heidelberg, and spent time working in Spain and the UK before finally settling in the West of Ireland, publishing poems in a number of collections in Ireland and the UK between occasional teaching jobs.

Fairly extensive travel for work and pleasure has been a leitmotiv in much of the work, as has the Western seaboard.

Contents

SHADOW BIRDS

Ice Core Sample

Brittle slices of back-time
Reveal ten thousand Springs,
Countless snowfalls and volcanic ash
Frozen echoes of a world
Men's minds did not embrace,
Not then, not now.

In lucite layers
Fern pollen rests,
Dust from pre-time
When the world was unwitnessed.

The past is reassembled,
Much like the truth in myths,
From fine grains and guesswork –
From echoes and old, old snow.

Voyaging

We buried her today;
No! That is not it,
We just folded away her coat,
Put it reverently in its box.

In truth, we drew in her mooring lines,
All the tugs and tenders
Had inched her out from the sea wall;
She was already under way.

She seems connected still,
But she is heading for open water,
Her canvas rattling up her mast.
Set on the timeless voyage.

For a long time we will see
Her sails in our spyglass,
Bright-work shining in the sun,
And her own flag crackling
In a wind we cannot hear.

Strangest Voyage
(Jonah's Captain Remembers)

The worst voyage you ask?
The one for Tarshish, without doubt;
We never arrived – were lucky to survive,
Excepting that little man –
He came to me as the last amphorae
Were stowed in the hold –
Had no destination, just *far away*,
Wherever trade took us.
I asked was it justice he fled –
Only God he replied.

He drank much of our sweet Syrian wine,
A lonely toper – too short with words and temper.
When he came among the oarsmen, we let him be.

Three days out of Joppa a storm broke –
Screaming demons from the North East.
Sea upon sea piled waves upon waves
So fast we lost our oars and mast –
The ropes and rails broke – or we cut them loose.
He stayed below, cursing, furious,
As if that wildness was his alone.

Howling days and nights dissolved together,
And our cargoes shifted like caged beasts;
First we tossed away the sacks of wheat,
Then pressed dates, apricots and fat olives
And only worse it grew; last we offered up
The precious jars of oil and Autumn wine.

Heavens! How we prayed – our cracked lips making
Supplications to all the gods we knew.

Through the fury that little man slept!
Hell's noise never stirred him
While my men, black eyes shot through
With blood and fear, faces limned grey with salt,
Were tossed like chaff in this the worst of storms;
And he slept! The helmsman shook him up,
Shouted to him to invoke his God, all ours had failed.
He came up to the slanting, sea-soaked deck,
Calm as rock, yelled out that this tempest was his
     reward –
How so? we asked. He told some tale of going and not
     going
To Nineveh, of running from his God –
All so long ago now, I can't be sure – but this I know:
He said we must give him to the sea, toss him away,
And we'd all be saved. We knew the sea's claim on us
Was close now, but still we feared to do this thing;
Each man begged forgiveness for the deed,
Then, as the ship heeled, we rolled him,
Unbound, silent into the long-fingered wash.

A moment later we saw a wild school
Of great, dark whales racing and
Diving in the cavernous waves:
As they dipped away the wind fell slack –
In less than an hour it came soft from the South
Calming the sea to a sleeping snake.
Not one man spoke a word.

Five days we took creeping up to Cyprus,
Much longer for the abject scenes replaying
Our sweaty fears of death to fade.
We spent all Winter fitting fresh mast and spars,
Repairing the hull and broken helm;
Bargaining with hard-eyed harbour men
For new stores and stock.

But strangest of all to me, I swear
I saw that little man once more
Boarding an East-bound boat.

Private Collection for Eleanor

Smooth, Mellifluous, Quickly, Elliptical,
Whisk, Jasper, Nuance, Merry and Blessed,
Cerulean, Ripple, Occipital, Russell, Lithe,
Camellia, Swift, Lucid and Tickle.

These words are for you –
Stemless flowers
Floating in a shallow dish.
Nothing to tell
Of their past – no future;
Now they rest on paper,
Up-turned faces,
Soft and full of my love.

Sound

The eight notes of an ugly clock
As it leaks time like an agèd tap,
Change a mood faster than the heart beats.

A slow saxophone, a distant mower,
Sirens, or wind in the chimney,
All raise their fears or speed the pulse,
In the thousand ways that only scent evokes.

Salix [Willows]

Salix, Sally, Sallow,
goat, gray, downy, crack.
Will you, will I, willow.
Long, green, browny, black,
reed bed, shore side, shallow.
Red twig, dead twig, bog,
catkins, bud-burst, leaf fray.
Sun shaft, wind blast, fog,
Siskins, love songs, linnets play,
Wrens nest in your hollow log.

Travellers

No blossom on the apple yet
But the first swallow came today.
Long before the First Temple
Gave fine-grained cedar beams
For fixing their mud homesteads
These aerobats raked the North-West sky
Swimming their ancient routes
Through the high, thin air.

Taking the earth beneath our feet,
To colonise palaces and caves,
They briefly turn them all
To cluttered noisy crèches;
Then, gathering before last leaf-fall,
Stream south to the Valley of the Kings
For the rich clouds of gnats
Rising from lotus ponds
Long before Joseph was in Egypt.

Bad Choice

So there she was – Eve – in the garden
Happy as a deep-water clam;
Then came this reptilian question:
'Would you rather be happy or clever?'
'Clever!' she said, without a thought
As to why they might be
Exclusive, one from another.

After that terrible lesson,
She learned what 'happy' had been;
But there is no unknowing
And nothing was ever the same.

No more garden now,
But clever enough to run from snakes.

Plane Leaves

Golden plane leaves scattered
Amid the dull November crowds,
Generous memories of hot, dry days
Cover the chewing gum and trash.

A swaddled form hunches in a world
Of tattered bags and deep disquiet,
Her thin hands full of last Summer
Swivelling the yellow leaf-stems,
The only brightness in her short day.

Recalling

When I think of you
I see your pale poet's face;
Palm pressed to your olive skin,
Breath caught inward rushing
And your indefinable eyes,
Hard-edged thought at their centre,
Bright with unasked questions.
But your self entirely eludes me.
How did your face fold round a smile?
What was it about your soft voice?
Why are your hands so clear
While your laugh is missing?

Hooligan

Heavy with salt, the wind
Paints my windows opaque –
Bends iron-hard hawthorns,
Strips clean a sycamore and
Heaps flower heads and plastic
Alongside the door.

Sweeping away a world of colour,
This tyro, that trashed my sleep –
Wrecked the shade and shelters,
Teasing and quiescent now –
Rascals up the lawn once more
To ruffle my hair, whisper into empty bags,
Before leaving the scene of the crime.

Lichen

Glacier slow, lichen builds obsessive maps
On stone and bark, detailed as fractals.
Tiny complex surveys in silver, grey and black.

They mirror in minutiae the shrew's path,
The hare's lane at meadow margin.
Will some future race discern
They were the map of a less destructive star?

When they have vanished quiescently as they came,
The air will no longer be fit to breathe;
These ancient barometers of our progress
Needed far more than we knew,
Will record our heedless folly
By one last act of absence.

Hands

Hands never lie,
They can't: sit on them,
Clasp or clench them,
Their life's work is clear.

Skin crumples to tissue,
Bone joints thicken or waste,
Quicksilver fingers falter,
Still, hands don't deceive.

If they hold a flensing blade,
Flutter a fan, drive straight nails
Or roll back a peach skin,
Each task makes its mark.

Eyes may be averted,
Smiles contrived, deceits concealed,
But the smallest acts are mapped
On the creased skin of your palms.

Hands never lie.

Accounting

We were spendthrifts of time,
Having a wealth of it
We gave it no value
Squandered it all away.

Innocence lost was ever irretrievable.
How could we value a state
We knew only by its absence?

Yours was a bankruptcy,
And mine a foreclosure.
Accounting's an empty pursuit.

After The Fall

By the time patience had mended the urn
It was far stronger than before
But too marked by repair.
No one cared to plant it again
With white roses or trailing thyme.

Half filled with last leaves and Winter rain,
For a year a sour soup fermented there;
Then, beneath the unchecked weeds
Robins made a Summer home,
And songs grew in its quiet heart again.

A Little Song for Ash Trees

The grey and green beauty of them,
The restless, elegant form they take,
The black and filigree dusk of them,
The late-leafing, airy shift of them,
The sun-threaded Summer face of them,
The light lemon hem at their leaf-fall.

The smooth twigs in the youth of them,
The rough bark Time carves on them,
The clean lines Winter makes of them,
The wind-whipped turmoil when they're tall;
My heart whirls off with the keys of them,
Oldest or youngest, such joy in them all.

Previously Owned

I, a Möbius strip of DNA.
Am all my myriad forbears;
Jew and Gentile, Pirate, Judge,
Good-wife, Maid and Saint,
Hero, Harpy, the dispossessed;
Tender of plants, breaker of hearts.

Threads of all these lives
Breathe to my heart or break to my will,
All that I am was some other's once,
Rough hair and hands, my face, my skin;
Yet am I an unrepeatable event,
More than mere proof by my presence?

Slow Learner

After you left for good,
For a while, I curled up
In a small corner of my body,
Too cold to move my mind around.

People shouted to me
But in that fog, I thought
They addressed someone else,
And continued to crouch as time trickled by.

One day I resumed the search,
Braving preliminary dives
In those cold, old shallows –
Chill as my own chilled self.

I swam deeper in familiar waters
Searching, but not for you,
Wanting the lost puzzle pieces,
Losing all perspective in a sunless world.

You always knew what sent me off,
Wasting my strength in the cold;
Told me the simple truth,
But now water drummed in my ears.

You recommended handstands in the daisies,
Letting the wind wash my face, and
No more diving after what lies only
In the province of the dead.

Old Anger

Not knowing you were missing
No search was made;
Anger too long submerged,
Loses its distinguishing features.
Its time came to surface,
Washed up on a high Spring tide,

Lonely as all dead things –
Waiting for answers and burial,
Unrecognised, unclaimed.
What could you have changed
If you had not been held face down,
Long ago before the reasons also drowned?

Trust

In my voyaging and my travels
I am kept forever faithful
Amidst the fitful freedoms
By your ever absent arms;
And in the restless nights alone
My spirit waits reunion,
My other half of reason.

After travels, the quiet that is love stabile.
Cupped in your smooth palm my cheek warms,
In wonder I traced your joining at nose and chin –
The sound of shared breath
Two silences that speak such peace.
You know I cannot leave you
For you always let me go.

Requiem for a Sailor

The years together we awaited re-fitting weather,
The perfect days to lay on the last coat of lacquer,
Days of heat that dry the early dew,
Still, warm days for coats of translucent varnish;
They would come, like leap years, finally they would
    come.
Patiently new things were found and old things
    renewed,
And still the weather refused our will to settle.
The new moon brought at last the fine and settled run,
And Summer strung one perfect drying day to another:
But early on the morn of St. John's Eve you sat up
Coughing, no more than other mornings,
And changed the destination of our lives for ever.

Deep in your skull some small thing broke,
Your blood silently formed a dark spider.
For open-ended ever we sought to placate it,
Until my blood seemed the only offering left,
But it would have none of it, and swinging hope hung
    still.
It was unsated 'til your strength was all used up;
Then, too tired to struggle, wrapped in its web,
Slowly, without a sigh, every part of you gave in.

You'd spoken with your eyes and your agile hands
But freedom and speech were all destroyed;
The avenues of escape closed, though sometimes
You voyaged to places still, in your mind,

Swimming in phosphorescent seas,
Drawing and drinking and rolling a smoke;
Randomly retrieving shipfuls of land-falls and laughter,
Cuba and Catalonia, Connemara and Tangiers, your
life's short haul.

On a wild November day, like the Ark of the Flood,
The small grey church held such varied friends and
debtors.

Did you laugh at the unfamiliar meeting place for us
all?
The suit I wore for our formal parting
Was the same I wore to our first meeting.
Life's not a ledger and I falter at the symmetry.

On our wedding day which of us laughing lovers
Foresaw my solo struggle against a turning tide?
Rowing those dead-heavy ashes, once my soft-whistling
sailor,
Spilling them to slant through a rough, indifferent sea.
You are so utterly gone I cannot dream of you
Nor remember your voice, always too soft for strangers.
We thought ourselves set to voyage the waters of the
world
But, like your dust, our plans sank slowly away.
Alone I am so much less than one,
Like a glove when the hand is withdrawn,
Where before we were more than our sum;
Gone now our ship-shaped retreat.

Though once more I drift to new seas,
Now it's the Sargasso of a waterlogged heart
Awash with your unfulfilled dreams.

Afterwards

The wild strawberry I swallowed
I should have bitten and slowly dissolved;
Careless, I always expected others.
Returning another day, all I found
Were blackened fruits, rotting
After long soaking nights and cold.
How could I know it was the last?

I never recalled the taste of our last loving,
Did not know it was a leave-taking.
Now we would know to savour each other,
Look into the dark iris' throat,
Stop for the song of the Spring flood,
Not swallow our senses, wait for them to melt us.
How could I know it was the last?

The Quick or the Dead

Rush to brief Beauty,
Stop for nothing else;
She's a transitory gift –
A breath-stopping balm.

Lose not a second,
Your soul's at stake;
Break the sound barrier,
Barely touch ground.

She needs no witnesses,
Only for a moment she dyes
The day's plain cloth –
Bending sunlight through rain drops.

Miss the boat for her,
Skip what you must,
She will move the furniture
Painting light in your head.

Retreat

The old monk left me
The whole wide world it seems,
And all the quiet day to read
Its mood in the Summer heat.

The warm wind tossed hedge trees –
Seaweed in a great sea swell –
And three small, piercing birds
Pursued a thousand flies.

Dark cows at anchor, dismasted hulks
Awash in a green and silver sea,
Ignored the tattered crows
Longing for winter's plough.

Ceaseless, collar doves nag
In the soft, flaked beeches.
Dull Sitkas drape a far-off hill,
Churchless spires in the noon time haze.

The stream moves silently,
Only fleeing debris betrays its speed;
Determined fish face the current,
Mirrored above in damselflies.

Over the untreed bank,
Threaded with mint and dock,
Bees scribble noise on the lank air,
Echo of their short lives' work.

On an alder's casual limb
A kingfisher adjusts his suit,
Then, faster than fear, strikes and is gone
While dragonflies duel in the dappled light.

Ecclesiastical yews hold heat
In their scented depths, spreading memory
Of incense to wind-washed meadows –
Empty as Eden after the Fall.

Twelve Noon

Walking past an open window
The Angelus follows me,
Like a cold wind,
Up the empty street.
Echoing back
To a hospital ward
Where this bell summoned
Rushing professionals
To postpone, but not prevent
A death as hard as any crucifixion.
I was beyond hearing
When the news followed.

West Mayo

Big-boned, laughing men ridged those lazy beds,
And daily growing leaner, took them sky-wards;

Now shaved by a hundred years of sheep
The soft green ribs belie the fiercest war
Ever waged and lost in these hills.
Revealed in the clear September light
They are the corrugations of old hunger
On the thin-skinned hills.

'West Mayo' is a very local poem about the potato 'lazy beds' – a ridged soil
cultivation system used here because of the rain. At the time of the worsening
famine in the 1840s, people tried frantically to dig these potato 'lazy beds' higher
and higher up the hills, hoping to avoid the blight which was rotting the chief food
source at the time.

Changing Boundaries

The sea shucks off deceptive calm
Returning to its ageless destiny
Paired with the wildness of wind.

Flinging its jaws at coast lines
Grinding sheer cliffs to shingle;
Grasping back its dominion
As fields move to dunes, then vanish.

Recalling time when water ruled –
This vast, restless beast braces
For re-invasion; a world once more
All silt and submersion.

Old Sweetness

The Ogen, skin a textured net,
Opens to translucent green,
Laced with smooth, flat pips,
Full of sweet juice transpired
    from the Jordan;
A synthesis of lead-heavy heat
With dusty soil, old
Before Abraham and Sarah
Came up from Ur;
For a moment I am eating the Promised Land.

Last Shot

(*St John*, Ch. 21)

All night a wind, no moon,
Hauling the nets by torchlight,
Over and over again – nothing.
To the East day draws the first line,
On the North shore small flames flicker;
As they draw nearer a man calls them
To shoot their nets once more to starboard.

The sky over Moab lightens fast now,
Whilst they land such a seething catch
That two thousand years on we still know
Their odd number and wonder at the untorn nets.

On a great flat rock, half awash,
That bright fire invited men in
From the restless dark, to break their fast,
Warm themselves after the long night,
Start a new day joyfully.

Failed Diplomacy

In the dark I signed invisible treaties with you,
Hoping for mutual concord.
When you rang from far away
I imagined your famous smile –

It irradiated the rest of my day.
Your letters were my dispatches,
Sent back from East and West
Mapping new territories.

Your last posting was a fast leave-taking;
Communiqués arrived too rarely,
I would not look at the lengthening space –
The sign of diplomatic shift.

Far away you initialled another alliance;
This was the real treaty
You announced one sunless day,
Wishing to share your joy with an old ally.

I offered my congratulations –
As is done with all such unions,
Informed the relevant parties,
Quietly accepted renewed isolation.

Lost Track

Old rail tracks like older canals
Follow contours,
Folds of walking land;
Roads, life's business now,
Have taken other routes.

Long untravelled by trains,
Flowers homestead the old sleepers.
Footfalls vanish in the green,
Soft as time passing.
Skittish calves and quiet cows
Meander haunch high
Through meadow sweet.

Like old bones, tracks run
Side by side to nowhere –
Raising the formless ghosts
Of earlier times, unmarked by
The lives that hurried once this way
Long spent and unremembered.

Mare

The green smoke of April
Clings to the blackthorn hedge;
A grey mare stands in its lee,
Resigned, still, her kohl-dark eyes
As sad as a harem houri.
Her Spring and Summer foals
Long vanished down the lane.

This heir of an ancient herd,
Once heart-beat of the Steppes
Faster than a blizzard
And fierce as Tartary,
Waits out the late cold
Hoping now only for oats.

First School

Looking at the thin scar
I recall the Nuns' neat playground
Hopscotch and skipping ropes,
The skidding run and headlong fall
Iodine's smell and searing bite.

The harsh hand-bell gathered us,
A plimsolled crocodile in Holy Mary blue,
Then scattered us to high-windowed rooms
Two by two at the slope-topped desks,
Each with an inky rut for our wilful pens
Whose nibs splayed, gushed, or turned ghost
With random spite, staining our small hands.

A favoured one carried round
The blue-lipped jug, always overfilling
The white china inkwells.
Slowly we learned to use our pink blotters
To draw off the spilled and splattered ink.
As haste made hurricanes
On the narrow-margined page,
It absorbed more than the sour-smelling ink –
Despair grew on its blurred boarders,
As African exports eluded me
And I dreamed of my Bakelite lunch-box.

Chalk dust danced in the afternoon sun
Whilst tomorrow's spellings multiplied like germs,
Squealing across the dreary blackboard,
Set to swallow playtime after the long ride home,
And the battle scar proudly revealed.

1950

When I was young there were always smart,
Cat-eyed women who talked too fast,
Dragging deeply on filter cigarettes,
One eyebrow arched, believing nothing,
Watching everything like city sea-gulls.

With depression and war for play-ground,
Those restless connivers surfaced,
Rewriting the social signposts,
To include 'Survive no matter what'
Dispatch gentility with a cynical grin.

They laughed pity at their mothers,
Encased in elastic and bone,
Gloves that always matched their shoes,
Thick-ankled pillars of modesty,
Clinging to manners and thrift.

These Sirens in Chanel suits
Exploited every asset but constancy.
Plum-lacquered their fingers and toes
Changing husbands or lovers like
The length of their hem (for better
Or worse, but never for poorer).

But their offspring tried flower power,
Sit-ins for freedom and choice.
Swapped high-tailored fashions for
Long skirts and flares from Indian stalls;
'Coming out' was not about dressing for balls.

Trapped between depression and decadence,
Their tans still perfect, their hair always done,
Those sharp-tongued survivors
Found no comfort in anarchy or dope –
Lifting their glasses they drank to their war.

Bipolar Blues

You can always see when Lily isn't flying,
All the signs are there –
She loafs around the foyer –
No destination in her eyes
And too much baggage for a trip;
Bright colours thrown aside,
Hands without rings,
Cheerful ear-rings left behind
Just fog on the runways;
Someone calls her flight but
Lily doesn't hear because,
Without doubt, today,
Lily isn't flying.

Waking Up

In the alluvial mud
Below the black lake
Where the unsettling dust
Of all days is distorted by depth,
The pendulum is on the rise:
Aeon slow, ascending to the warm shallows
Where the cloudy water and grey land
Invite no glad arrival
And only an act of imagination
Propels the sleeper into morning.

Stolen Curiosities

My mind is a jackdaw's nest
Tricked out with things to wonder at:
The hottest white dwarf,
The largest Black Hole,
The greatest elliptical orbit,
Sparks and quarks and double helix,
Treasures all of a piece.
Reason alone its reason for being;
Dazzled by simplicity –
Transfixed by complexity.

The huge patterns revealed
In the smallest details;
The spider's spiral
Filled out in the sea snail's shell.
The tree's self-heal
Echoes the lizard's lost tail.

When my mind is an empty nest
And all the world's a blizzard,
Ah! then curiosity drops
one more glittering delight
and frozen will, self forgetting,
Re-awakes to wonder.

Last Prisoner of War
(Japanese soldier found in remote jungle 1984)

The Emperor's last warrior
Perfectly concealed by shadows,
Listens to the menacing quiet,
Dressed only in a shroud of obedience,
Prepared for the expected end.
Habits, tight as jungle vines, first nature now:
Self-denying duty survived his last comrade.

Not relief, but the ordinary world
Stumbles on this battle-ready relic.
Disarmed by change beyond imagining,
He steps from a pool of lost time,
Blinking in camera lights,
Finds more than his war is lost
And that this grief will not pass.

How to live time at ease now,
See new things with his old eyes?
Often longing for war's certainty,
He holds his breath in readiness
Again, waiting for the last stand.
His grandsons laugh softly.

Shadow Birds

The mist is lifting and
Hidden houses come clear again,
The shadows of swallows
Scythe across a white wall –

For a moment there is no present,
Just the pressure between a past
And an unfolding –
A point with no mass:

Like shadows and mist.

Broken Heart [To my mother]

After her funeral I broke the china heart –
A powder-dish with flowers on the lid,
A gift of my sixth Summer to
A czarina wrapped in crepe de Chine.

She performed her transformation
Many evenings before her triple mirror.
Sapphire-eyed and shimmering,
Varnishing her nails to match her brilliant lips.

Already she seemed far away –
A dream, and I the dreamer
Left inhaling the scent of her
Powder pressed on my cheeks,
As she went her way to somewhere else.

Now and Then

Far over the river
Water-colour houses, neat as tulips,
Hold hands below
Freshly ironed hills
Sporting one tree
Tipping its hat to the wind.

A couple of aeons ago
Glaciers shape-shifted
Sharp rock ridges here;
Left footholds for
Clots of dark firs, then
Brambles, birch and bracken –
For wolves and giant red deer.

But wind and ten thousand years of rain
Softened and smoothed it all to this –
A safe and pretty place –
Home to rooks and rabbits,
Not ready for the next change.

Salad Bowl [Call to a Simple Feast]

In this blue dish, a world:
Pale avocado slices
Ripened on a scorched kibbutz,
Shredded carrot from the Lutheran lowlands
Mix with apple-dice picked in orchards
Where it is already tomorrow,
And damp raisins soak up the royal blood
Of beets harvested by solemn Poles,
As they have for a thousand years.

The hot-headed scallions
And soft-hearted greens –
Gifts from a small farm –
Gleam with the oil of Spanish olives
And sharp French cider spiked
With garlic, pepper and coarse crystals
From shining salt pans far to the south,
Crushed and ground together;
Harmony, in this blue dish at least.

Winter Room

My heart is a Winter room
In a glorious Summerhouse.
Pale dustsheets conceal
Domestic details;
Sad light-denying blinds
Cancel all the colours;
Its magic carpet
Rolled against the wall
And only dusty spiders
Arabesque across the floor.

It waits for Winter to leave,
The owner to return,
Flooding the room with colour,
Dancing with armfuls
Of Summer's scented flowers.

Pentecostal Wind in Jerusalem

In that upper room,
Now void of furnishings,
Seven dry leaves swirl
In a small wind –
The ghost of one
That blew away all
Fearful doubts –
And blowing still,
Draws us from our
Empty inner rooms
To search and hope.

The Diagnosis

They went together,
Lock-stepping into the office.
The brown desk, the hard chairs
Protected the sayer of sooths
From human mess;
Crossing his short legs
His stone words spill over his polished shoes.

She sat, a marble Madonna;
He, forgetting to breathe,
Becalmed in the pale light fading.
Before her eyes the future breaks,
Sharp splinters scatter in her lap,
As darkness streams through
Tomorrow's shattered window.

For a while yet he will not soak up
The mossy smell of his mortality;
Wanting to tamp more sand on the sand-castle
Unready to face the rising tide or
Hear the silent scream, not of gulls
But her, keening for lost time.

Leaving the executioner,
Slow-stepping now, out of rhythm –
His head a magnet for normal things,
Proof life's still open for business.
Her's, a vortex sucking in the dark.

Part of her trying to fix the game,
Mark the cards, send the sun back up the steps.

The future has arrived, he must learn
A minute scale, but not quite now.
She, already storing his warmth, his scent,
Does not look into his eyes –
Keeping to herself the reflection
Of that Wintertime coming
To walk beside her –
Sleep in her empty bed.

Moonrise

Wrapped in late Winter light
the pale wafer rises
in the evening's dawn,
spilling lemon stains
down the rippled tide
to its still-water hem.
And last birds
chase infinity
beyond compass points.

Well, Can You?

Holding in your eye
the first fish to breathe air
and the last man standing,
all that emerged and failed,
You love us still

Knowing the seventy
rain-washed Winters that
prepare the soil to clothe
our quick crumbling remains,
You love us still

Seeing how men tired
of hand-to-hand killing
and deftly learned to
slaughter whole tribes at once,
You love us still

Hearing women beg,
wheedle or quietly pray,
hearts full of bargaining,
small thanks an afterthought,
You love us still

But for the children
we find a hundred ways
to twist or crush or lose,
for their small, broken lives –
Can you love us still?

For My Daughter

You still have much to do
Searching the ocean's edge.
I've started the move inland
To higher ground.

Your essence is centred on ardent work,
Your bright soul must roll up its sleeves,
Whilst mine folds its hands.
You hold the future, we accept it thus.

My blood-work is done and
My heart enjoys a kind of peace,
That province I doubted long to find;
I live well with uncertainties now.

Your heart's squeezed by the world's promise
And the fear of doubt.
We reach across love and loss,
The waiting and hoping and pain.

And still you have much to do.

Just Another Extraordinary Day

Just another extraordinary day,
Six finches exploded by one glance from the cat;
A silver moth turned into silver bark;
It rained noisily for ninety seconds, I counted.
Millions of people moved through the air,
Rising to unimaginable heights.
No news of my friends,
But some people agreed peace is a good thing.

My face took an hour to unfold this morning,
After missing trains and losing luggage all night.
The tap water tastes of pencil sharpenings;
Ants are carrying off greenfly to milk them –
Imagine that, a greenfly dairy.
There is an outbreak of small men
Bullying whole countries again,
And my cousins in America are still asleep.

New Widow

For too long she wing-walked,
Kept aloft by up-drafts of
Brave and wilful hope.
Then, the harsh encounter
With unfeeling ground again.

Now she sits, freezing in the sun,
An empty smile propped
On her empty face.
Mind racing from memories
Like a horse refusing the bit.

She cannot open the press,
The clothes there smell of him,
His writing on a fly-leaf stops her heart,
And small sketches – lethal traps that
Swallow whole afternoons;

Now time runs in more than one direction –
But *Now* is not a place she wants to be.

Another Fatality

Her phone rang too early,
At this hour it could only
Be the worst news, now
Embodied in a formal voice;
Too much to accept yet.

In a dozen blurred days
His put-together body came home
In his stiff dress uniform,
His pride still shining on the buttons
And smart black belt.

Companions came, uneasy, reserved,
Fired a volley above his open grave,
An echo of the last sound he heard.
She put away her good teacups
While his sister dried the glasses.

Wandering around the emptiness
With nothing left to do – not ever –
She cocked his impeccable cap
On her looking-glass stand,
Slipping his picture below –

His lovely, laughing face flat
In the mirror's corner, as cold
And smooth as his cool grey cheek.
Now half her reflection
Will always be lost beneath his.

Autumn Cat

A half grown jigsaw
Of cream and Autumn colours,
She followed us, dancing
Down the quiet lane.

Forests and fields in pale light,
Her world growing larger
In our moving shadows –
Too large we thought,
Turning our way towards home;
But dog-magic made her vanish.

For two long days I called her
In half hope, along the dark tree-line,
Listening for the smallest trace –
At last she whispered back.

I carried her home,
A swirl of soft singing gears
Stitching thanks on my heart.

My Father and Me

Your easel was angled for light
From the long North windows,
A brush in your hand and one in your teeth,
The patchwork palette hooked on your thumb
And silver paint tubes lying about
Like tired soldiers without their caps.

My farmyard spread beneath the table
Near the hissing gas stove,
Twig and plaster hedges between bright, coloured
    fields.
Maker of weather, I painted Spring into Winter,
Placed the lead livestock in seasonal danger,
Then set them in Summer meadows on a whim.

Our effortless peace drew you in.
Cancelling all worries with
Your fast flying pallet-knife,
Conjuring huge rolling skies over
Boisterous seas full of light,
Or kindly, brown country, empty and wet.

Sometimes you whistled a phrase or two –
Then, leaving the ducks on looking-glass pond,
I would wind the old gramophone
And we'd sing all the music we knew;
Making and changing our weather,
Painting our wished for worlds.

Land Loss

Once the common land was enclosed
The good and the bad striped wisely no more,
The shared work turned day-long labour;
The old ways of change destroyed,
The spiral of response unravelled.
No greater group remained to hold the line
Against the sweep of logical progression
Taking captive family and farmland.

Where once dairy, pond and great elms thrived
Block houses cover land first farmed in Saxon times.
Here tired commuters in their city suits
Fear for their aimless, cold-eyed young –
Testing their savvy swinging from railings,
Fearless of lorries, confounded by cows –
Who never stole a warm hen's egg,
Saw the year's first lamb, heard the pig's last scream.

Put away now, the old survivors
Sit alone beside cups of sweet tea
Serviced in shifts by professional carers.
The seasons' inaudible rhythms
No longer define their life's limits;
These last years spent amongst strangers
Recalling their uncommon pasts.

Autumn in Aigues-Mortes

The low stone house,
On a small parcel of land,
Close to the water course,
Is quiet by itself
In the arms of a willow;

Half dressed in ivy
Where the sun is checked
By tall, dry rushes
Conspiring together
At every wind's breath;

On a seat, three rough stones
By the old planked door,
Six late butterflies
Settle, circle and rise,
In the last Gavotte of the day.

With a sharp handclap
I drive off two magpies –
Raucous ruffians –
Soon returned to stamp their feet,
Fracture the Autumn peace.

Winter is still just a rumour
In the gold grass and dark red vines.

Words

Each word has its own atomic weight,
Their countless formulae unlimited.
Today I have misplaced my scales, and
Wrongly-guessed weights combine
To form unbalanced thoughts.

I could write words vivid as sheet lightning,
Strong as soot, that might remain unread
For twelve generations, then new eyes perceive –
A window opens, the thread winds on.
What once I saw may yet be seen again.

Which other sentient creature, ardent egoist,
Gives to the future records of lust and despair,
The alchemy of loneliness or perfection?
Another light gives words such variance
Drawing from them balm or bitter ice-blasts.

Weighted or weightless
Their alphabets allowed us, alone,
To leave observations across time,
That ripple for a season, then fade,
Reborn with meanings beyond any
Dreamed at their inception.